How to Fire Your Boss & Start a Business...After 40

The "I Quit" Workbook

Copyright © 2017 by Cheryl A. Mauldin

Elite Women in Business
1 Willow Creek Lane, #1202
Jonesboro, AR 72404

Ordering Information:
Quantity sales. Special discounts are available on quantity purchases by corporations, associations, and others. For details, contact the publisher at the address above.
Orders by U.S. trade bookstores and wholesalers. Please contact 870-219-6504.

Printed and published in the United States of America

ISBN 978-0-9993822-1-9

First Edition

This workbook is the companion to the book, "How to Fire Your Boss & Start a Business...After 40", and contains all the exercises outlined in the book, links to additional resources and the business start-up checklist.

Use the workbook to follow along as you read the book, with ample space to complete the exercises and take notes.

Get the book now on Amazon!

Link: http://bit.ly/Fireyourbossbook

Dear Future Elite Woman in Business,

*Thank you for purchasing the I Quit Workbook! It truly means a lot to me, because one of my core values in both life and business is **impact**. And, I hope that I can share my experience on how I built a multiple six-figure business within a few years, so that you can do this, too!*

This workbook is the companion to the book, "How To Fire Your Boss and Start a Business…After 40. While you can certainly complete all the exercises in the book without the book, it was designed to complement the book by completing as you learn each strategy in the book. If you did not buy the book, you can get a copy at **http://bit.ly/Fireyourbossbook**

It's my hope that I can make an impact by helping as many women as possible find the freedom to resign from their burnt-out professional career and start a business that is genuinely profitable and purposeful. If you're reading this and you're one of those women, I'd love for you to create the life you've always dreamed of living through the insights and practices you find here.

*If you're new to me, I'm the founder and CEO of **Elite Women in Business**, the company I built just shy of my 50th birthday, through which I offer one-on-one and group coaching services to help women over 40 learn how to take their business idea and launch a purpose-driven, profitable business.*

After spending decades slogging it day-by-day in the corporate world, I now have the freedom to set my own schedule, choose my own clients, create limitless income, and most joyfully, give back to the causes I most believe in.

Best of all, I can travel and enjoy time with my daughters — as I'm about to become a grandmother for the first time, I can say that spending time with my daughters and soon grandchildren are one of the most rewarding parts about being a thriving female entrepreneur.

Know this as you start your journey, there are no magic-bullets or trade secrets to be a successful entrepreneur. Overnight success is a myth; it rarely happens. Get-rich-quick schemes only make the person selling those rich. You will not find any of those in this book. I am committed to providing you with proven strategies that I and other successful entrepreneurs have used to build a successful and profitable business.

Here's to your success!

Cheryl Mauldin

Contents

Separate yourself from 99% of the population by completing this entire workbook. The difference between dreamers and doers – is doers take action. Consistently day after day, those that are blazing trails and accomplishing their dreams are taking action.

If you have comments or questions, jump over to the ELITE Women in Business Facebook community at http://elitewomeninbusiness.club.

You might look at where I am now and think that it's been easy to get here. In many ways, it has — in other ways, I was forced into it. (Thankfully.) I'll share a little about how my journey unfolded, so you can understand how your path towards entrepreneurship can lead to great success quicker than you think, too!

Though I've technically been an entrepreneur since the age of 18, running side photography businesses while I worked in "Corporate America", I wouldn't have necessarily called myself a successful business woman, because I found myself working seven days a week, sometimes from sun-up to sunset.

And, even with a nursing and business degree that eventually led me to become the Chief Quality Officer of a company owned by a Fortune 500 Corporation, I still found myself in six figure debt as a single mother.

I spent 24 years with that organization, 15 of which were as a C-Suite Execute, but I was completely burned out, lost my passion, and felt completely trapped.

I was 49 years old.

My comfortable salary kept me trapped, because no matter what business idea floated through my mind, I had a huge fear of failing my daughters.

Five years after I moved into the C-Suite, I realized my job wasn't right for me anymore, but I stayed on for another decade. I made sacrifices, willingly, to provide a comfortable life for my daughters and give them every advantage I could. I'm not at all resentful, because I'm a devoted parent, and know that it was the right decision to make at the time.

I simply wish I would've known long ago that I could transfer my skills into a consultancy practice that would give me so much more enjoyment – doing many of the same things I was already doing – and earn three times what I had been making before.

So, I kept on. Then, early in 2015, my company was sold and reorganized. After devoted service to my corporation, I was immediately demoted three layers deep in middle management with a huge pay cut and substantial loss of benefits.

How was I going to live the same lifestyle now that I was making less money?

How could I align myself with a new mission statement for a company I didn't care about?

What was I going to do now that my daughters were grown?

I spent the prior year mentoring with Darren Hardy, publisher of *Success Magazine*, both through his free daily emails and paid programs. Somewhere in my heart, I knew I wanted to become a full-time entrepreneur, to pursue the path I had started when I was 18, so I began to take small deliberate actions in that direction.

I knew I needed to leave my job. I could not *continue* to do the same thing every single day anymore, let alone spend another decade and a half of my life there. I did not want to learn how to work with a new executive and management team. Worse still, I didn't want to simply find another job doing the same thing for a different company — my passion was gone. I was burned out. I was no longer challenged.

I felt like I could not get off this treadmill.

Yet, in the past, my part-time businesses had consumed my life. I only knew how to work *for* my business, rather than *on* my business, and no matter how hard I racked my brain, I could not figure out how to replace my corporate salary.

Then, one day, I had a crazy idea. What if I took the skills, knowledge and experience from my corporate career and simply started a consulting business? After all, I was considered an expert in the field.

What if this could actually work out…?

I thought about this for two days. Journaled. Did some research. Prayed. Then on the third day, I received a mentoring email from Darren that said, *"Do it today. Do something incredible. It could be something that you have always wanted to do, but have been a bit chicken to try. Yep, don't wait another day, do it today. That is what a mentor is for, to push you to do what you know you should do, but no one has pushed you to stretch to your full capability. It's okay if you are scared – do it scared. But do it! The thing you know you should do. Just do it now. Do it today."*

"The thing you know you should do. Just do it now. Do it today." – those words echoed through me. I could not stop thinking about the message. I knew at that moment what I had to do.

I walked into work that morning and wrote my resignation letter.

All I had was an idea. Still, I decided it was worth pursuing and after turning in my resignation letter, I have never looked back.

Over the course of finishing my required thirty days with the organization, I did everything you'll find in this book to create the business of my dreams, craft a plan for my life that I would ultimately truly enjoy living, and create my plan to become financially free.

If you follow the steps in this book, I believe you can do it, too.

I was 49 years old when I got started and by some standards, I was "too old" to start anew. Some people thought I was crazy. Some people thought it was a terrible mistake. But, with my children out of the nest and a dismal corporate future ahead of me, I was motivated beyond belief to make my OWN business a success.

I was driven by my core values to create impact and provide service.

I was inspired by the mentors I followed.

I was inspired by the people I would be able to help.

I was impassioned to create my dream life, for me and my family.

Were there bumps in the road? Of course.

Was every day easy? Of course not.

An entrepreneur's journey is more like a rollercoaster than a walk in the park. There are ups, downs, twists and turns. Every successful entrepreneur goes through failure and success. We learn from failure and celebrate success.

As often happens when you begin to follow your dreams, I began to notice there were so many other women like me, trapped in careers they felt they would have to stay in until retirement. They were resentful they were passed over for promotions to people with less experience and fewer skills. They were tired of trying to compete with younger and more energetic co-workers, just to get noticed. They made the same sacrifices I had made for their families, but in their heart of hearts they knew they were meant for more.

Is this how you feel, too?

Along with the book, "How To Fire Your Boss and Start a Business…After 40, you hold in your hands the beginning of your road map to be open for business – in a business that you own and operate. From beginning to end, you should be able to craft a roadmap for your very own business idea, so that you can go from "I wonder…" to "Open for business!"

It doesn't matter where you complete the exercises, in the book or workbook, or how long it takes you to do them — the most important part is that you actually do them! This book is designed to take you where you want to go, but only if you do the work.

An article in Entrepreneur magazine estimates that only 8% of the population pursues personal development. An article in the Atlantic estimates, of those who sign up for personal development (like reading this book, enrolling in an online course, etc.), only 2% finish. Of that 2% only who finish, only a few will implement what they have learned.

The second compelling reason to not just read this book, but also take notes and complete the exercises can be found in the Forgetting Curve. Research on the forgetting curve shows that within one hour, people will have forgotten an average of fifty percent of the information. Within twenty-four hours, they have forgotten an average of seventy percent of new information, and within a week, forgetting claims an average of ninety percent of it.

Over the past few years, I have learned the difference between highly successful business women and women who want a successful business is that truly successful women *act*. They take massive action, even if it means facing their own fears.

That's why it's helpful to have a coach to guide you along. And, that's what I'm here for!

Now, let's build the business of your dreams!

"If you have ideas, you have the main asset you need, and there isn't any limit to what you can do with your business and your life." – Harvey S. Firestone

The key to success for any business, any product, any service is that you offer something that people want (or need) and are willing to pay for. This is often a solution to a problem they have or perceive they have. By our very nature, entrepreneurs are all problem-solvers at our core.

Every business provides some type of solution to a problem, real or perceived, the customer has. The trilogy of business success comes when you do something you are good at, something you are passionate about, and something your customer needs or wants (and is willing to pay for). The sweet spot is where these intersect.

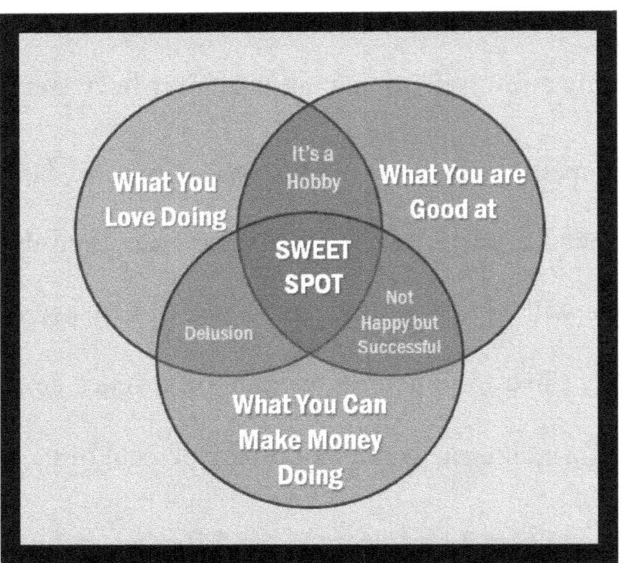

Your Extraordinary Exercise

Extraordinary visions ignite your soul, fill you with energy and joy, and allow your life to be filled with purpose and passion. Unique abilities are your mastery level skills that align with those visions to make it reality in your life — only if you follow that extraordinary vision. These are the things you cannot help but do.

Write down what you are an expert in, what you do well. (If you get stuck, ask a friend.)

What is your passion? What do you love to do?

What are your unique abilities? Not just the things you are good at, but the skills and knowledge that you cannot help but do, the ones that fill you with passion, that spark your creative side, and fill you up with enthusiasm and energy?

Write a description of your business idea(s):

How does your business idea align with what you are passionate about? What you are good at? What you love doing? What you are an expert in?

Is your business an online business? Or a brick-and-mortar business? Or something else, like home / garage / hobby shed?

Describe the type of products or services you want to offer:

Describe what you believe your customers problem to be solved or need/want is:

Describe how you can make this a successful business, by what you are good at, what you enjoy doing, and what you are passionate about:

How do you know if you are on track?

Good question. There are two key elements you need to work on:

1) Who is your customer?

2) Does your product or service resonate with your customer? (a.k.a., would they pay you to provide the solution to their problem?)

"You cannot make everyone happy. You are not pizza." – Neelabh Shandilya

Your ideal customer is the person who will pay for your product or service, and become a raving fan of your business. You cannot target everyone. You cannot fulfill the needs and wants of every person on the planet. This is where attention to detail becomes important, and an investment in the homework of this chapter is worth so much.

Your goal is to identify who is your ideal customer to know: who are you targeting?

You are crafting a person with as much information and detail as possible. This is not about statistics and demographics of a group. Statistics are valuable when getting to know your audience, but creating an individual avatar helps in all your decision-making.

Use the space below to develop your ideal customer avatar. It does not have to be pretty! Just brain dump everything you can find out about your perfect customer.

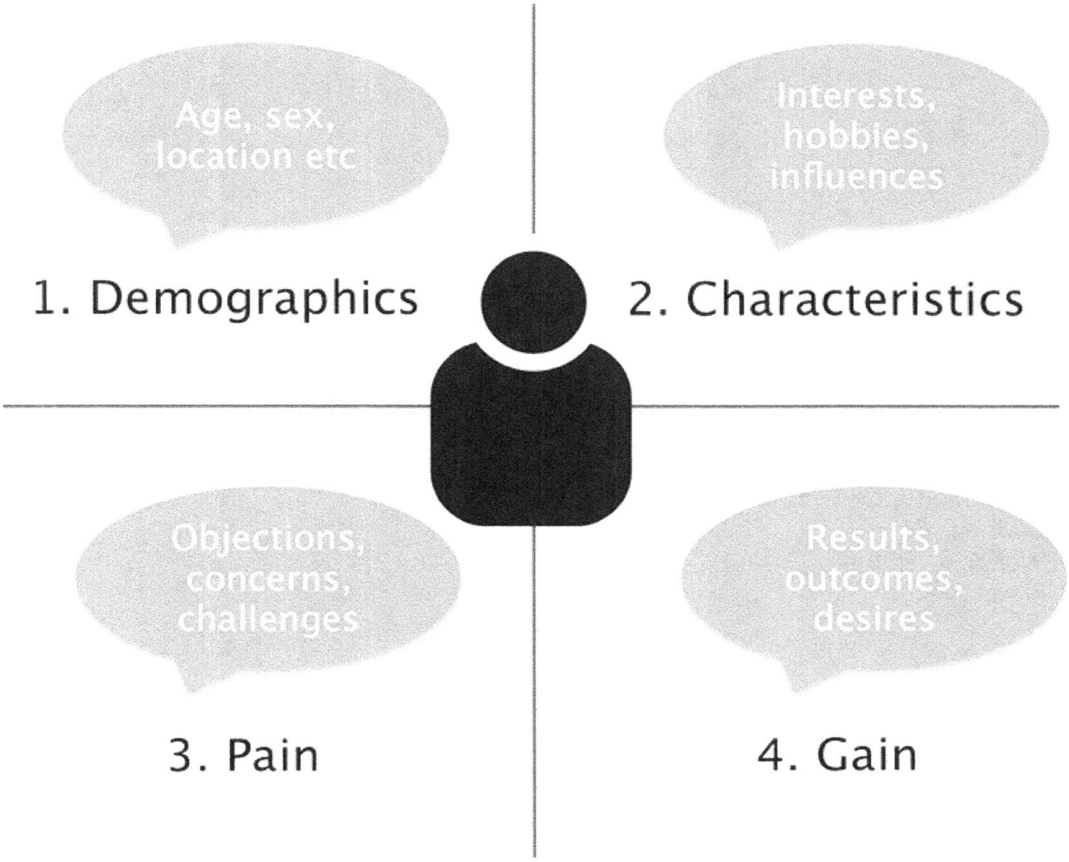

4 Dimensional Customer Avatar

Name

Demographics
- Age:
- Gender:
- Salary:
- Location:
- Education:
- Family:

Hobbies/Interests
- Hobby:
- Hobby:
- Interest:
- Interest:

Goals & Challenges
- Primary Goal:
- Secondary Goal:
- How We Help:
- Primary Challenge:
- Secondary Challenge:
- How We Help:

Values & Fears
- Primary Values:
- Primary Fears of Doing Business With You:
- How We Help:
- Primary Challenge:
- Secondary Challenge:
- How We Help:

Social Media Channels
Active on:
Belongs to groups:
How active:

You can also download a customer avatar worksheet at http://bit.ly/fireyourbosstools

At this point, you have an idea of an offer, whether it be a product or service. You have developed the story of your ideal customer. **The next step is crucial.**

If you skip this step, you risk investing time, money and energy into launching a business that may not succeed!

A good business idea is only a good idea if the customer thinks it is a good idea. A great business idea is only a great idea if the customer is willing to pay you.

It's time to test your idea in the marketplace, which is considered pre-launch and pre-development.

What did you learn about your ideal customer's use of social media?

During interviews of your ideal customer, use the following types of questions. Develop some of your own questions related to your business or product / service idea. Then record what you learned below.

- *Have you ever paid money to solve this problem?*
- *What factors do you consider when purchasing a product or service like this?*
- *What do you like or dislike about current products or services currently on the market?*
- *What areas would you suggest for improvement?*

- *How much would you pay for this product or service?*

- *Your question:* ____?

- *Your question:* ____?

- *Your question:* ____?

Interview #1

Name: ____

Feedback:

Interview #2

Name: ____

Feedback:

Interview #3

Name: ____

Feedback:

Interview #4

Name: ____

Feedback:

Interview #5

Name: ____

Feedback:

(You can record additional interviews and market research in the NOTES section at the end of the workbook)

Common themes or similarities among the interviews:

What does my competitor do well?

What do current customers say about my competitor's business, product or service? Look at testimonials and reviews?

What is the competitor not doing well? In my opinion? Based on the market research you did. Look at testimonials or customer feedback.

What weaknesses do you notice? In their store front or web presence? In their marketing message? With their products or services? In customer service? In pricing? Look at everything. Your competitor's weakness is your opportunity.

Now, critically compare you versus them. How can you be better? How are you already better? How can you be different and unique? How can you solve the customer's need in a way not being solved by the competitor? What can you offer they are not and do it better? What makes you unique?

Core values are what you fundamentally believe. They help you determine if you are on the right path and fulfilling your business goals. Core values create an unwavering and unchanging guide for you as the business owner.

Below you will find a list of examples of core values:

Above and Beyond	Dependability	Individuality	Reason
Acceptance	Depth	Industry	Recognition
Accessibility	Determination	Informal	Recreation
Accomplishment	Determined	Innovation	Refined
Accountability	Development	Innovative	Reflection
Accuracy	Devotion	Inquisitive	Relationships
Accurate	Devout	Insight	Relaxation
Achievement	Different	Insightful	Reliability
Activity	Differentiation	Inspiration	Reliable
Adaptability	Dignity	Integrity	Resilience
Adventure	Diligence	Intelligence	Resolute
Adventurous	Direct	Intensity	Resolution
Affection	Directness	International	Resolve
Affective	Discipline	Intuition	Resourceful
Aggressive	Discovery	Intuitive	Resourcefulness
Agility	Discretion	Invention	Respect
Aggressiveness	Diversity	Investing	Respect for Others
Alert	Dominance	Investment	Respect for the Individual
Alertness	Down-to-Earth	Inviting	Responsibility
Altruism	Dreaming	Irreverence	Responsiveness
Ambition	Drive	Irreverent	Rest
Amusement	Duty	Joy	Restraint
Anti-Bureaucratic	Eagerness	Justice	Results
Anticipate	Ease of Use	Kindness	Results-Oriented

Anticipation	Economy	Knowledge	Reverence
Anti-Corporate	Education	Leadership	Rigor
Appreciation	Effective	Learning	Risk
Approachability	Effectiveness	Legal	Risk Taking
Approachable	Efficiency	Level-Headed	Rule of Law
Assertive	Efficient	Liberty	Sacrifice
Assertiveness	Elegance	Listening	Safety
Attention to Detail	Empathy	Lively	Sanitary
Attentive	Employees	Local	Satisfaction
Attentiveness	Empower	Logic	Security
Availability	Empowering	Longevity	Self-Awareness
Available	Encouragement	Love	Self-Motivation
Awareness	Endurance	Loyalty	Self-Responsibility
Balance	Energy	Mastery	Self-Control
Beauty	Engagement	Maturity	Self-Directed
Being the Best	Enjoyment	Maximizing	Selfless
Belonging	Entertainment	Maximum Utilization	Self-Reliance
Best	Enthusiasm	Meaning	Sense of Humor
Best People	Entrepreneurship	Meekness	Sensitivity
Bold	Environment	Mellow	Serenity
Boldness	Equality	Members	Serious
Bravery	Equitable	Merit	Service
Brilliance	Ethical	Meritocracy	Shared Prosperity
Brilliant	Exceed Expectations	Meticulous	Sharing
Calm	Excellence	Mindful	Shrewd
Calmness	Excitement	Moderation	Significance
Candor	Exciting	Modesty	Silence
Capability	Exhilarating	Motivation	Silliness
Capable	Exuberance	Mystery	Simplicity
Careful	Experience	Neatness	Sincerity
Carefulness	Expertise	Nerve	Skill
Caring	Exploration	No Bureaucracy	Skillfulness

Certainty	Explore	Obedience	Smart
Challenge	Expressive	Open	Solitude
Change	Extrovert	Open-Minded	Speed
Character	Fairness	Openness	Spirit
Charity	Faith	Optimism	Spirituality
Cheerful	Faithfulness	Order	Spontaneous
Citizenship	Family	Organization	Stability
Clean	Family Atmosphere	Original	Standardization
Cleanliness	Famous	Originality	Status
Clear	Fashion	Outrageous	Stealth
Clear-Minded	Fast	Partnership	Stewardship
Clever	Fearless	Passion	Strength
Clients	Ferocious	Patience	Structure
Collaboration	Fidelity	Patient-Centered	Succeed
Comfort	Fierce	Patient-Focused	Success
Commitment	Firm	Patients	Support
Common Sense	Fitness	Patient-Satisfaction	Surprise
Communication	Flair	Patriotism	Sustainability
Community	Flexibility	Peace	Sympathy
Compassion	Flexible	People	Synergy
Competence	Fluency	Perception	Systemization
Competency	Focus	Perceptive	Talent
Competition	Focus on Future	Perfection	Teamwork
Competitive	Foresight	Performance	Temperance
Completion	Formal	Perseverance	Thankful
Composure	Fortitude	Persistence	Thorough
Comprehensive	Freedom	Personal Development	Thoughtful
Concentration	Fresh	Personal Growth	Timeliness
Concern for Others	Fresh Ideas	Persuasive	Timely
Confidence	Friendly	Philanthropy	Tolerance
Confidential	Friendship	Play	Tough

Confidentiality	Frugality	Playfulness	Toughness
Conformity	Fun	Pleasantness	Traditional
Connection	Generosity	Poise	Training
Consciousness	Genius	Polish	Tranquility
Consistency	Giving	Popularity	Transparency
Content	Global	Positive	Trust
Contentment	Goodness	Potency	Trustworthy
Continuity	Goodwill	Potential	Truth
Continuous Improvement	Gratitude	Power	Understanding
Contribution	Great	Powerful	Unflappable
Control	Greatness	Practical	Unique
Conviction	Growth	Pragmatic	Uniqueness
Cooperation	Guidance	Precise	Unity
Coordination	Happiness	Precision	Universal
Cordiality	Hard Work	Prepared	Useful
Correct	Harmony	Preservation	Utility
Courage	Health	Pride	Valor
Courtesy	Heart	Privacy	Value
Craftiness	Helpful	Proactive	Value Creation
Craftsmanship	Heroism	Proactively	Variety
Creation	History	Productivity	Victorious
Creative	Holiness	Profane	Victory
Creativity	Honesty	Professionalism	Vigor
Credibility	Honor	Profitability	Virtue
Cunning	Hope	Profits	Vision
Curiosity	Hopeful	Progress	Vital
Customer Focus	Hospitality	Prosperity	Vitality
Customer Satisfaction	Humble	Prudence	Warmth
Customer Service	Humility	Punctuality	Watchful
Customers	Humor	Purity	Watchfulness
Daring	Hygiene	Pursue	Wealth

Decency	Imagination	Pursuit	Welcoming
Decisive	Impact	Quality	Willfulness
Decisiveness	Impartial	Quality of Work	Winning
Dedication	Impious	Rational	Wisdom
Delight	Improvement	Real	Wonder
Democratic	Independence	Realistic	Worldwide

Defining Your Core Values

Invariably your business core values typically align with your personal set of values. In looking through this list, what resonates with you immediately? Which ones speak to you and what you want to create?

Write as many values as you identify with below:

Narrow the list to at least three values, which become THE core values for your business.

Next, let's work on the vision for your business. Your vision will provide your provision. The vision statement relates to looking ahead, outlines your business goals and where you are headed. Your vision statement outlines how you help people, the value you offer, and what you plan to achieve as a business. It is written in plain language that is meaningful to you, your customers, and to any future employees.

If you choose to create a vision board, put a photo of it or a print of it inside your workbook. And, please share with me on Facebook at this link: http://elitewomeninbusiness.club

Write your vision statement here, don't try to make it perfect:

Your mission statement explains what your business must do day-to-day to make your vision statement a reality. It is in the present tense. Any time you wonder, "What should I do today" or "How should I act today?", you can turn to your mission statement for guidance.

A mission statement is a few short sentences or paragraphs outlining what your business does to achieve its vision statement.

Look at your vision statement and ask yourself, "What must I do to make this a reality?" Mission statements should be customer-focused, so a better question is, "what must I do for my customers to make this vision a reality?"

A well-developed mission statement Is a great tool for understanding, developing and communicating your fundamental business objectives. A mission statement will answer questions like the following. Answer these for your business.

Who is your company?

What do you do?

What do you stand for?

Why do you do what you do?

What market are you serving?

What benefits do you offer?

What problem do you solve? Or, what luxury do you provide?

What culture do you create for employees?

Write your mission statement here:

"You cannot build a dream on a foundation of sand. To weather the test of storms, it must be cemented in the heart with uncompromising conviction." - — T.F. Hodge

Just like building a house, your business needs a solid foundation to be successful and sustainable. This is the business building stage to get you from business idea to open for business. Creating a business that meets legal requirements, that begins with a strong financial foundation, provides protection for the business owner, and looks and feels like a real business are the cornerstones for a sustainable and profitable business.

What's in A Name?

Let's start with the basics: naming your business and operating a legal business.

Business naming checklist:

- ☐ I love this business name
- ☐ My target market loves this business name or I feel the name will resonate with my ideal customer
- ☐ The business name is clear
- ☐ The domain name in .com, .net, .org, and .club are available
- ☐ The Facebook page for this name is available
- ☐ The Instagram page for this name is available
- ☐ The Pinterest page for this name is available
- ☐ The twitter page for this name is available
- ☐ There are no other corporations using this name
- ☐ There are no other LLC's using this name

Is your business name you chose good to go? Or, do you need to go back to the drawing board?

After going through the checklist, getting feedback, and doing market research my business name will be:

You basically have the following choices for the legal structure of your business:

- *Sole proprietorship (a single owner)*

- *Partnership (more than one owner)*

- *Limited Liability Corporation (LLC)*

- *C-Corporation (Inc.)*

- *S-Corporation (Inc.)*

Sole Proprietorship	General Partnership
Advantages: • Minimum legal restrictions • Ease of formation • Low start-up costs • Sole ownership of profits • Maximum freedom in decision-making	Advantages: • Ease of formation • Direct rewards • Broader management base due to greater number of owners
Disadvantages: • Unlimited liability • Less available capital • Relative difficulty in obtaining long-term financing	Disadvantages: • Unlimited liability of general partners • Divided authority
No. of Owners Allowed: Only 1 owner	No. of Owners Allowed: At least 2; no upper limits
Taxation Issues: • Not subject to federal income tax at entity level; tax items reported on Schedule C of owner's personal return	Taxation Issues: • Not subject to federal income tax at entity level; tax items passed through to the partners
Formation • File DBA (doing business as) • Will need Federal Identification Number if any employees	Formation • Partnership agreement • May need Federal Identification Number from IRS • Each state may have filing requirements

Notes:

Limited Partnership	Limited Liability Corporation
Advantages: • Ease of formation • Direct rewards • Broader management base due to greater number of owners	Advantages: • Can have a single-member LLC (a disregarded entity) • Limited disclosure of owners • No advance IRS filings • Ease in transfer of ownership • Can use different classes of owners • Lower filing fees
Disadvantages: • Unlimited liability of general partners • Divided authority • Difficulty disposing of limited partnership interest	Disadvantages: • Large numbers of owners complicate status • Death, bankruptcy or withdrawal of owner can cause problems • Doing business in other states may require filing individual tax returns in each state
No. of Owners Allowed: • At least 1 general partner and 1 limited partner • No upper limits	No. of Owners Allowed: • At least 1 general partner and 1 limited partner • No upper limits
Taxation Issues: Not subject to federal income tax at entity level; tax items passed through to the partners	Taxation Issues: Not subject to federal income tax at entity level; tax items passed through to the partners
Filing and Formation: • Certificate of limited partnership • May need Federal Identification Number from IRS • Each state may have required filings	Filing and Formation: • Articles of Incorporation • May need Federal Identification Number from IRS • Each state may have required filings

Notes:

C-Corporation	S-Corporation
Advantages: • Separate legal entity • Limited liability for stockholders • Unlimited life of business • Relative ease in raising capital • Transfer of ownership through sale of stock • Can use different classes of stock	Advantages: • Limited liability for shareholders • Unlimited life of business
Disadvantages: • Organizational complexity • Expense activities limited by charter • Extensive regulation, record-keeping requirements • Double taxation of profits and dividends	Disadvantages: • Restrictions on number and type of shareholders • Limitations on classes of stock that may be issued
No. of Owners Allowed: • At least 1 • No upper limits	No. of Owners Allowed: • At least 1 • Upper limit is 75
Taxation Issues: Subject to federal income tax at entity level and upon shareholders when receive dividends	Taxation Issues: • Not subject to federal income tax at entity level • Tax items passed through to shareholders
Liquidation: Taxable to corporation and shareholders to extent distribution exceeds stock basis	Liquidation: Generally non-taxable at corporate level and taxable at shareholder level to extent distribution exceeds stock basis
Filing and Formation: • Articles of Incorporation • Federal Identification Number from IRS • Each state has required filings	Filing and Formation: • Articles of Incorporation • Federal Identification Number from IRS • Filing with IRS to classify as S-Corporation • Each state has required filings

Notes:

Here is a resource where you can obtain information specific to your state in relation to requirements and filing: https://www.incorporate.com/choosing_a_state.html

What business structure did you choose?

Requirements for your state:

Appointment date / time with my accountant or tax preparer: _______________________

Appointment date / time with my attorney: _______________________________________

- [ ] Meet with accountant to discuss which business structure will best suit your business

- [ ] Meet with an attorney for assistance in creating bylaws and articles of Incorporation, if you choose an LLC, S-Corporation or C-Corporation

- [ ] Hire your attorney to serve as your registered agent, if filing C or S Corporation

- [ ] Apply for local licenses required

- [ ] Apply for county licenses required, if applicable

- [ ] Apply for Doing Business As (DBA) with city and / or county, if required

- [ ] Apply for state registrations or Incorporation, if applicable

- [ ] Apply for IRS classification as S-Corporation, if applicable

- [ ] Apply for IRS Federal Employer Identification Number, if applicable

- [ ] Apply for state sales tax certificate, if selling physical products that require sales taxation

- [ ] Complete all local and state requirements to operate a business for your specific state

- [ ] Register with your state for state withholding of Income taxes of payroll for yourself and any employees

- [ ] Register with your state for unemployment Insurance withholding of payroll

- [ ] Register with your state for required workman's compensation withholding of payroll

- [ ] Register with the state for FICA withholding of payroll

- [ ] Open an account with a payroll service to handle your payroll, or ask your accountant to offer the service

● ● ●

I am currently debt-free? YES / NO

If your business is already open, do you have business debt? YES / NO

What limiting beliefs or difficulties with money do you have?

What do you remember hearing from your family as you grew up about money?

Write your "get out of debt" plan here: (Download a free template at http://bit.ly/fireyourbosstools)

Action Step #1: From your very first day as an entrepreneur, **never ever mix your personal and business finances.** This requires a separate bank account for your business. If you have a DBA (doing business as), a partnership or any of the other legal business structures, you will have the necessary paperwork for the bank to open the account.

- ☐ Business bank account opened

- ☐ Set up your invoice templates.

- ☐ Develop contracts.

- ☐ In the beginning, you may also opt to utilize Square, Stripe or PayPal to collect payments, in addition to personal checks.
  - o This will allow you to accept credit and debit card payments, at a reasonable rate. The preference for you will be made based on if you have a brick-and-mortar business or online business.

- ☐ Credit card processing system (Remember, in the early days of your business, you most likely do not need a credit card processing system beyond these three methods. Only take on additional expenses when they become necessary.)

● ● ●

Download a budget template in Microsoft Excel format **at this link:**

http://bit.ly/fireyourbosstools

Here are some financial considerations for your start-up budget:

- *Cost of meeting with accountant and setting up your bookkeeping chart of accounts*

- *Cost of meeting with attorney*

- *Application fees for licenses, registrations, incorporations, etc.*

- *Writing articles of incorporation and corporation bylaws, if establishing a C-corporation or S-corporation*

- *Insurance policies*

- *Domain name registrations*

- *Website hosting plan, if a website is required*

- *Business checks*

- *Rent or lease payments for brick-and-mortar spaces*

- *All required equipment (notice the word "required")*

- *All required supplies (notice the word "required")*

- *Perhaps business cards — these are not the mainstay they used to be*

- *Quarterly income taxes*

Every business will have its own unique start-up expenses. Your accountant should be able to help you plan for your business. The Small Business Administration is also a great resource for start-up budgets.

I offer more in-depth education and resources for the financial aspects of your business in the

ELITE Business Building Foundations eCourse – get more information here

https://elite-courses.thinkific.com/courses/elite-foundations

"A brand is the set of expectations, memories, stories and relationships that, taken together,

account for a consumer's decision to choose your product or service over another." – Seth

Godin

Customers aren't looking for another cookie-cutter company who offers the same thing as everyone else. They are looking for an experience tailored to their needs, backed by genuine personal interaction. This is why branding is so important.

Now, it's time to define your brand as a *person,* rather than as a logo or a written voice. If your company were a person, what type of person would that be? How would that person present themselves? How would they behave? How would they speak? How would this person gain the trust and support of the ideal customer?

Brainstorm here:

What colors do you feel express your brand? (It is totally okay to go off to Pinterest and have a look around the mood boards)

If you are artsy, do you have a concept for your logo? Sketch that here or write down the must-haves to communicate to your logo designer.

While you are at it, pick a font that you will always use in every piece of information or communication: (Later you can choose a second or third to add in, let's stay basic right now). You can do a web search for fonts to see examples and try out typing your business name to see how it will look.

Hint: You can see how your business name will look in a specific font by opening a Microsoft Word document and clicking through the various fonts, until you find one you like. You can also find fonts for free 1001 Free Fonts, https://www.1001freefonts.com/

Here is a great article on the Fast Company blog about the psychology of colors and business.

(https://www.fastcompany.com/3028378/what-your-logos-color-says-about-your-company-infographic)

Which colors represent your brand? *The* Pantone website (https://www.pantone.com/) *is great for color research, as well as Pinterest. On Pinterest, search for mood boards. Feel free to print pictures to include here.*

Your business brand color palette:

How will you incorporate your brand colors into the brand?

Describe how you want to interact with customers:

Describe what you want the customer experience to feel like to the customer:

If you will deliver physical products, what does the brand packaging look like:

If you will own a storefront, what does it look like? What does it smell like? What is the arrangement or décor of the space?

What Is the personality of the brand? (Formal, Informal, quirky, authoritative, collaborative, comical, etc.)

Where are your people? Where is "your person"? What social media sites does your ideal customer use regularly?

- ☐ Facebook

- ☐ Twitter

- ☐ Instagram

- ☐ Pinterest

- ☐ YouTube

- ☐ Snapchat

- ☐ LinkedIn

- ☐ Marco Polo

- ☐ Other: ____________________________

Your social media accounts and usernames:

- ☐ Facebook: ____

- ☐ Twitter: ____

- ☐ Instagram: ____

- ☐ Pinterest: ____

- ☐ YouTube: ____

- ☐ Snapchat: ____

- ☐ LinkedIn: ____

- ☐ Marco Polo: ____

- ☐ Other: ____

I hope you finish the book and workbook and the pages are highlighted, written on, and folded over. I wrote it for that specific purpose. Through all my years as an entrepreneur I can honestly say I did not always do business the right way. But one thing I did do right is to try to learn from my mistakes.

One of the biggest mistakes I made for most of my entrepreneurial life was to just try to do everything alone, which has taught me two valuable lessons:

One, doing it the hard way does not make you a hero. It makes you stubborn. Staying in my zone of genius makes me a happier and more productive, and profitable entrepreneur.

Two, building a business on a solid foundation with an intentional plan, not only for the business, but also for my life was one of the best decisions I have ever made. Looking back and comparing my photography business with my current businesses, there is no comparison.

I really had no life before. No time for family. No time for friends. No time for fun. No time to take care of myself. Stress, anxiety, debt, non-stop work – you could barely call it a life.

When I became a full-time entrepreneur, I spent time asking myself questions about the kind of life I wanted to live. I went about creating a business that fit into that plan after I knew the answers.

My life today looks very different. I regularly take time off, and at least one day every week is a completely unplugged day, where I fully disconnect from all things business and do whatever I want.

I have been blessed that I was able to take my whole family on several adventures this year. We cruised the Caribbean over Christmas and New Year's, saw a throw-back 90's pop group in Vegas this spring, and just visited Alaska and British Columbia. I don't say that to brag. I tell you this to highlight the importance of making time for what you love. For me, that is my family and travel. The memories and experiences we have shared the last two years – I cannot even begin to put a price tag on it. Like the commercial says… Priceless!

My lifestyle today allows time for creative projects, rest, exercise, family, friends, travel – all the things that are important to me. I have a plan for my life and my business. I plan for taxes and annual business expenses. I plan for business emergencies. I plan for profit. And, I plan for me.

All of this is possible because I focused first on building a solid business foundation. I then concentrated on eliminating my personal debt. And finally, I designed my business to fit into that kind of lifestyle.

Is every day smooth sailing? Of course not. But, just like the nursery rhyme, my business can withstand a few setbacks and "storms" because the foundation is solid.

I hope you have used this workbook to get your business open, whether that means your quit your day job and went full-time. Or, you started a brilliant side business. We have literally walked through every step of the process to open your business together aside from product creation, which is beyond the scope of this book. The exact steps I followed to launch my six-figure business.

The length of time it takes to launch your business will be different for everyone. I opened my consulting business within 30 days, while my coaching business took multiple months. Life, drive, dedication, learning, and opportunity all play a factor.

You may choose to leave the 9-to-5 behind and go all-in with opening a business. Or, you may choose to start a business on the side. Either way, you have a roadmap to launch your business into the world with this book.

I cannot wait to hear your success story!

Please email me WHEN your business is open and successful (cheryl@cherylmauldin.com), I want to feature success stories on my blog and social media, so be sure you let me know. I would also love to hear your feedback, struggles, and questions.

I'm beyond grateful any time I know I have helped another woman over 40 leave a burned-out career and create a profitable business. When I hear her say she is living a life she now loves, I'm over the moon.

So, please share your story with me.

Wishing you all the success in the world,

Cheryl

About the Author

Cheryl Mauldin is a business strategy coach, Founder of Elite Women in Business, CEO of Relentless Consulting, Inc., author and keynote speaker. She provides premium coaching services to women over 40 who are ready to leave their burned out 9 to 5 and create the business and life of their dreams. She has been featured in Success Magazine as a Thoughtleader ®, on the EOFire podcast and many other blogs and podcasts for entrepreneurs.

She lives in Arkansas, loves to travel, read, and photography. She is mom to three beautiful daughters, Brittany, Lindsay and Hannah.

Connect with Cheryl

Blog: http://cherylmauldin.com

Facebook: http://elitewomeninbusiness.club

Elite Women in Business Podcast

YouTube: http://elitewomen.tv

Twitter: http://www.twitter.com/cherylmauldin

Email: cheryl@cherylmauldin.com

Business Building Masterclass: **https://elite-courses.thinkific.com/**

Give me 12 weeks and I will show you how to build the business of your dreams!

Stop slugging it out day after day at an uninspiring, mentally draining job, and create the business of your dreams.

Be able to do the thing you were born to do – fulfill the purpose you were put on earth to do.

Launch your business on a solid foundation that is set up from day one to be profitable and help you achieve the lifestyle you want.

In my 12-week eCourse, ELITE Business Building Foundations you will get the tools and resources to make smart decisions in your business launch phase to set you up for success.

There is no fluff, no BS, no magic bullets, or unicorns. Just solid strategies and practical advise that I used to create multiple six-figure revenue in the business of my dreams.

My business has made the WORLD of difference to me, my family and the lives of the clients I work with.

Imagine how different your life would be if you could get up every morning and do work that inspires you, makes you feel alive, and is actually fun.

Imagine how different your life could be if you were pursuing and building your dream, instead of someone else's dream.

Imagine how different your life could be if you were in charge of how much money you generate, instead of depending on someone else to value your worth with an hourly wage or annual salary.

With over thirty years entrepreneurial experience, I know a thing of two about what works and what does not. I made my share of mistakes along the way and went through the business school of hard knocks.

Along the way, I have worked with some of the smartest minds in the entrepreneurial world, such as Darren Hardy and Stacy Tuschl. I have also invested tens of thousands of dollars in education, mentoring and coaching. I have been featured in Success Magainze, the EOFire podcast, and others for my business success and strategies.

Now I coach women over 40 who are trapped in the 9-to-5 game of trading time for dollars at a job they have grown to hate, but feel stuck. I help women just like you create their own brilliant lives and businesses. I run private coaching programs, group coaching programs, and host private retreats.

But, to you, none of that will mean anything until you take the first step. Until you are ready to invest in your own success and take action, not much is going to change for you.

It's okay if at this point you are scared, overwhelmed, and confused.

It's okay if you have no idea where to start.

It's okay if you feel like you have waited too late in life.

I was exactly where you are before I left Corporate America and created the business of my dreams. I was almost 50 years old, in debt, with little retirement saved, and felt trapped.

But I believed there was a better way and a better life. I knew I was meant to do more with my life. Had I not taken action and invested in myself, I would still be punching that time clock every Monday morning, working on someone else's dream.

It's time for you to make a decision.

Do you want more of the same old thing for the rest of your life? Going to work day in and day out facing the same frustrations, bumping your head against the glass ceiling, wondering how you will ever make it to retirement.

Or, are you ready to claim your greater purpose? Step up and create the life you know deep inside you were meant to live. Create a solid and profitable business doing what you love and what you are good at.

Trust me, your life will never be the same, and you will never look back and say "what if."

If you are ready to take the first step in creating your dream life, say YES to your life, say YES to creating your brilliant business, you are ready for ELITE Business Building Foundations.

https://elite-courses.thinkific.com/courses/elite-foundations

So, what's in the course?

- The exact blueprint I used to leave my 9-to-5 and launch a business
- Specific strategies for refining your business idea and doing market research
- How to niche down to your ideal customer

- Discovering your unique selling proposition
- Identifying strengths, weaknesses and opportunities
- Business structure
- How to build your business model and sales funnel
- Business finances and budget
- Making profit a priority
- Charging what you are worth
- Setting 100 day goals
- Designing your ideal life
- Money mindset
- Investing in your success

The full course is jam-packed with information, value, and BONUSES! We all love bonuses, right?

In this course, you'll receive:

• 12 Modules

• LIVE Q&A call

• Access to private Facebook Group

• Bonuses! And extra training

• Discounts to Future Live Events

Each lesson in the course comes with a value-packed workbook to help you get the most value from each lesson.

BONUS: There will be a free Q&A call mid-way through the course and at the end where you can pick me brain. These live calls are the perfect time to ask questions, validate your ideas, and go even deeper with your learning.

BONUS: As you finish this course, and wonder, what next? I'm giving you access to my own 8-week Launch Plan as a special bonus!

Plus, other exciting bonus content!

This course regularly sells for $1497.

For a limited time I am offering at only $997!

I know how intimidating it can be to launch your own endeavor, especially if you're a successful woman after the age of 40.

That's what kept me in a job I no longer loved for a decade too long.

It is also scary to jump in as an entrepreneur especially after you have built a comfortable life. Yet, that dream keeps playing over and over in your head.

I know, because it was the same for me.

I do not want you to hold yourself back any longer. Let's launch your brilliant business idea out into the world, and start creating a life you love. Once where you are excited to jump out of bed every day because you love what you do!

I designed this course for you! Let's do this!

Enroll today and save $500.

From business idea to launch in 12-weeks!

https://elite-courses.thinkific.com/courses/elite-foundations

Appendix I

Your Complete Business Start-up Checklist – Getting from Business Idea to Open for Business

- ❑ Have a Business Idea
- ❑ Do market research to test your business idea
- ❑ Select a business name
- ❑ Determine the core values for your business
- ❑ Write a vision statement for your business
- ❑ Write a mission statement for your business
- ❑ Write your business goals
- ❑ Develop your business budget
- ❑ Register domain names for your business
- ❑ Meet with accountant or tax preparer
- ❑ Determine the legal structure for your business
    - ❑ Sole Proprietorship
    - ❑ Partnership
    - ❑ Limited Liability Corporation (LLC)
    - ❑ C-Corporation
    - ❑ S-Corporation
- ❑ If owning a corporation, meet with attorney for filing assistance
- ❑ If owning an LLC or Corporation, develop the bylaws and Articles of Incorporation for the corporation
- ❑ If owning a Corporation, hire a registered agent
- ❑ Research state specific guidelines for operating a business in your state. https://www.incorporate.com/choosing_a_state.html
- ❑ If corporation, LLC or partnership: obtain a federal employer identification number (FEIN) from the IRS
- ❑ Open a business checking account
- ❑ File for federal and / or state trademark protection or patents, if necessary
- ❑ If seeking funding, write a formal business plan
- ❑ If necessary, lease office, warehouse or retail space
- ❑ If home-based, check local zoning requirements
- ❑ If you are manufacturing products, purchase product liability insurance
- ❑ Apply for necessary local licenses or permits
- ❑ Apply for necessary state licenses or permits
- ❑ Apply for necessary federal licenses or permits
- ❑ If you will sell a physical product, apply for a state sales tax certificate or permit
- ❑ If required, file a DBA (doing business as) with your city, county and / or state
- ❑ If required, register and create accounts with all required state agencies (determined by your business structure and state requirements)
    - ❑ Secretary of State
    - ❑ Unemployment Insurance

- ❑ Worker's compensation
- ❑ Purchase business insurance required – general liability minimally
- ❑ Purchase necessary personal insurance
  - ❑ Health insurance
  - ❑ Dental insurance
  - ❑ Vision insurance
  - ❑ Life insurance
  - ❑ Short-term disability insurance
  - ❑ Long-term disability insurance
- ❑ If home-based, call your property insurance carrier to determine if you need additional insurance
- ❑ Set up a system for bookkeeping
- ❑ Purchase accounting software or sign up for online accounting services
- ❑ Determine if you need to hire employees
- ❑ Determine how you will process payroll and pay payroll taxes (even if you are the only employee)
- ❑ Design a logo
- ❑ Determine brand colors
- ❑ Set up a website, landing page or blog
- ❑ Set up social media accounts
- ❑ Develop necessary contracts or agreements
- ❑ Develop templates for billing, quotes, invoices, statements, etc.
- ❑ Open accounts with needed suppliers, vendors or contractors
- ❑ Interview potential employees
- ❑ If hiring employees, write your policy and procedure manual
- ❑ Hire employee(s)
- ❑ Develop a marketing plan
- ❑ Develop operational systems and automations
- ❑ Hire a business coach or mentor
- ❑ Fire your boss
- ❑ Open for business

NOTES:

NOTES:

NOTES: